Queer/onthology

Homespun Poems of Interwoven Migration

Edited by Cori Bratby-Rudd and Ana Bernal

This is a work of fiction. Names, characters, places, and incidents either are the product of the author's imagination or are used fictitiously. Any resemblance to actual persons, living or dead, events, or locales is entirely coincidental.

Copyright © 2020 by Q Youth Foundation

All rights reserved. No part of this book may be reproduced or used in any manner without written permission of the copyright owner except for the use of quotations in a book review. For more information, email: Ana Bernal, ana@qyouthfoundation.org

First paperback edition July 2020

Book cover design and layout by Ana Bernal
Book design by Cori Bratby-Rudd

ISBN: 978-0-578-61928-6 (paperback)

www.qyouthfoundation.com

Q Youth Foundation is a 501c(3) non-profit organization that promotes LGBTQIA+ storytelling, playwriting and community advocacy by creating a safe space environment for youth and community members, we offer resources, education and outreach for the under-served LGBTQIA+ community.

IG: @QYouthFDN
FB: QYouthFoundation
www.QYouthFoundation.org

Influx Collectiv is a queer poetry reading series that connects LA based poets, promotes queer events, and provides a space and platform for queer creators and queer content. Influx is for audience members to hear stories that reflect their own, and for performers to find an audience that understands.

IG: @InfluxCollectiv
FB: influxcollectiv
www.influxcollectiv.org

Acknowledgements:

We would like to thank the Crystal Torres and Manuel Gonez of the Roybal Foundation for opening their doors to us at the Roybal Learning Center in East Los Angeles. A special thanks to librecht baker, Hadrian Shawn Miguel and Lorilyn Luong for being champions in fundraising for this project. And thanks to Influx Collective's Cori Bratby-Rudd for facilitating, connecting with the writers, and sharing their expertise in poetry.

The GoFund Me contributors and donors for Queering Poetry project, without you all we would not have been able to make this project possible.

Abe Zapata	Jonathan Caballeros
Adam Bernstein	Lauren Humphrey
Albus Wang	librecht baker
Amber LaFlamme	Lorna Luong
American Hecho	Matthew Loung
Anonymous Donors x5	Mark Patterson
Art Jimenez	MJ Brown
Asuka Hisa	Misael Alvarado
Cam L.	Moncho Alvarado
Corey Nakashima	Nancy Perez
dante alencastre	Nelson Luong
Darwin Godoy	Patrick Toomey
Delfin Facundo	Ruben Mendive
Diego & Gaël Solis	Salvador Bernal
Griselda Valdez	Valarie Zapata
Isabel N.	Xavier Brian Wallace

Forward

For the first time the Q Youth Foundation and Influx Collectiv's Queer Poetry Reading Series combined forces, selecting some of the best emerging LGBTQIA+ poets in Los Angeles County for our inaugural 8-week Queering Poetry Workshop and Creation Lab. Every Saturday, this group of writers had to wake up bright and early, sit and ponder enjambment, poetic form, & meter—and then were all required to write daily poems. This course was a challenge, it was not something one could simply glide through. I am incredibly proud and inspired by all of the poets whose work appears in *Queeronthology: Homespun from Interwoven Migrations*. As a community, we decided that this anthology would be organized into categories by theme. There are thus five sections: It begins in the mouth, Love (broadly), Progressions, Definitions, and Pre(judice) & Healing.

As the facilitator, I want to first acknowledge and thank all of these poets who humored my musings and went on CA Conrad inspired tree touching expeditions, who wrote sestinas for the first time, who showed up and took detailed notes on each other's poems, who read and critiqued, and who pushed themselves. All of the pieces you are about to read were first drafted in our workshop and were honed and edited ruthlessly. You will see poets playing with and in form, you will see poets creating new language, you will see the work of folks who have experienced trauma, discrimination, poverty, and hatred contemplating healing and confidently expressing a brave vulnerability about their many experiences as queer poets and as queer poets of color.

In this course our main guiding question was *what is queer poetry?* Something that seemed to at first have a clear definition became blurred as we discussed and developed our own constantly evolving interpretations of the concept. Is queer poetry anything written by a queer author? If so, how do we know it is queer (unless we already know the author)? Is queer poetry something explicit? Does it have to be known to be queer? Of course, queer can be explicit, but does it have to be? How can poetry become queer, as in, how can we, using the dictionary definition of queer as strangeness, make the poetry writing itself (not the content but the form) strange? How can we indicate queerness in the method/techniques of creations?

The truth is, it was extremely difficult to narrow a definition, and it seems that the unanimous agreement was that queer poetry is something that is quite difficult to define, it can be something explicit yet obscure, something blatant, something hidden, or something we might never be able to actively define.

As such, the poems that appear below range from overtly gay to seemingly not addressing sexuality at all. That being said, here is your cue, all of these poems are queer—can you find the clues?

Best,

Cori Bratby-Rudd
Co-founder and Director of Influx Collectiv

It begins in the mouth:

Ode to a Mouth (Specifically My Own)
Audrey Kuo

sideways bow on tabletop
string taut, ready to let fly
quick tongue-shaped twist of words

lurking in the corners
lines of mirth warn of
jokes lurching to burst forth

mischief half-smirk
still visible kid lays beneath
always eager to play

what this mouth came to do
is bring joy
(yes, in those other ways, too)

came to stir feelings
spark movement, lips part
reveal tender razor tongue

the healer waits behind
darts through jester-opened doorway
a portal through which is channeled

sharp truth straight from
ancestors and the earth
of what you, too, came to do

a vessel, an instrument
doorway to more knowing
blessed shaper of things

mouth comes to say: long beach and coffeville; southern california and south, south mixed with columbus, georgia and a few other places
librecht baker

i ate my mouth often
    like simmered holiday collard and mustard greens
    Lillie Mae grew in her carmelitos housing project's front yard
    and knifed into a sliver for easy eating her children
    and grandkids, who laughed like thunderstorms
i ate my mouth often
    so often it could only tell you
    what my coffeville, columbus, and Long
    Beach lineage tastes as
it's been covered by familial women
    the kind that has seen ghosts floating
    at the top of the closet, felt invisible pursed lips
    blow a gale on our right ear, and seen a glimmer
    of Glover stroll through the house, while
    wearing a fedora, 20 plus years later
    after he became an Egun
encouraged to not ask "why"
and seek curiosity's answers
but urged to defend the body
    i have never physically fought
    putting someone on the ground
    with angry body blows

      pulling forth blood as a crowd
      like me cheers, but i've pushed,
      screamed in possession, pain, loss,
      celebration, etc.
of belonging to a place(s)
      i've learned violence is part
      of my place like 1619 english
my voice passing a holy ghost
over my brown-pinkish lips are more
cracked and cratered than
coconut oil slippery slick and moist
      i don't drink the recommended
      two liters of water per day
      if i did,
      my pussy would smell as water
i learned to silently say
      nothing while crossing my arms
      across my "b" sometimes "c"
      breast cup siz like Lillie Mae and Gladys
      and i held strange
      experiences like newborns
      i've never partitioned and pushed
      forth
i practiced to silently say
      because i was born into and
      believed hushness was part of who

        i am/was – i let it waft as ritualistic
        tobacco smoke push upward
        by a dusty ceiling fan
never bellowing voices
        against misunderstandings
for more than 20 plus years of life
mouth was born to not say
so body began growing things
        extra flesh filled liquids
        liquids body could easily
        reabsorb, but refused for
        too many years of repeated
        silence
and those things clutched flesh
        like an unacknowledged memory
so body began starving itself
        of lungs breath
        constrict – constrict
        lungs from expansion until
        my eyes rolled upward
        not in possession, but due
        to lack of lack of oxygen to
        my brain until Lanette held
        a brown paper bag over
        nose and mouth after
        a nebulizer treatment – in

  her arms,
  as she mothered alone
  in this moment
  with a fearful crooked lip
  and a determination made of
  Black womxnness,
  her generous, wide deer eyes watching me
  i looked up seeing God(dess)
  matriarch, my mother saving me
  from death,
  an Egun title coming too early
so body began rejecting me
begging for me to never leave

i learned
those growths of not saying
those growths
of not saying
those
growths
of not
saying

without
shifting our lineage
of normally

not saying what should be
said

my mouth says a shift

Lip Smack
Hadrian Shawn Miguel

Open wide
I see you mouth full
Wide open, deep and gaping
Cavernous
Overflowing con sabor

A flavor burst
Soft & wet
Cherry-tinted
Kissable & quenched

Oh so, delectable you are
Tongue & cheek, make out-able
Smack dab in the middle
Like cracks & backs
Lickable

Opinionated
Garish
Quick to speaks its mind
And countless days it says too much
Foot in mouth
Gagging
Deep throat-able

Silence as a shield
Basin for my truth
Simple & sharp
With a few drips of honey
Swallowing
Laughingly funny

Charcoaled & white
Your favorite colors
Detoxifies & cleanse your palette

Brighten
Pearly white frighten
Tense & puckering up
Sputters & spatters with queerness
Smackable
Lip glossable
A typical day, not any less

Ode to my mouth
Albus Wang

dry
cracked
taste of blood
of silence
of corrected
of who the heck you think you are
tender, tender love, loving
healed, soft, delicate
patterns clearly with no haze
blue, green, pink and gold
all the color and sparkle show
no more silence, no more correction
the mouth says what every mouth
must say
authenticity, truth, and the real real real
no need to scare, prevent, or stop
just join my mouth
speak the truth and the only truth
see my mouth move all around
she her own self I can't stop
look at her closely and closer
see that holiness nowhere else
she uses own voice for the change
lip color furious full of say

Open Mouth
Lorilyn Luong

Do you remember the anticipation of others when they wanted
to hear your first words?
how we smiled to your smile
as you gurgled, cooed, babbled
how we encouraged the use of voice

Along the years
teeth in full set grind
vocal chords begin to freeze
moving from vibration to hesitation
when blood and the news confidently blame victim
This happened a long time ago. Why are you talking about it
now?
It's nothing. Be quiet.
It's this kind of interrogation and invalidation
that make you want to stop the vomit from leaving their lips

It is in the moments when the tongue is forced back
is when we want to speak the most
The saliva is dry
teeth not brushed from thoughts of
Why care?
upper and lower lip wired shut
the body shuts down
when there is more inhale of what others think
what others say should be
and no exhale of today is the day I do what I want
I will do what feels whole

You remember what it's like to smile again
to speak again
to laugh
to say I love you
after what's been broken
You once stood tall

then crawled when stomped on
pushed back into the womb
when they didn't believe
Was this the day your body turned into a grave?

It doesn't matter what others think happened or did not happen
as long as you know what happened
and that is facts

I want you to face the audience with confidence
I want you to unshackle this secret that binds you
I want you to remember why you relay the message
Power is given when silence no longer consumes
Let us start living again
What do you stand for?
What do you value?
What must be voiced?

Nobody anticipates the words that leave your body after
surviving abuse
but when the trauma is trapped
it knocks on the doors of your ribcage
demanding to be free
running the mountains of your lungs that wanted to breathe
again
swimming up the throat and safely landing on tongue
because your voice missed you
loving yourself

Love (broadly)

In The Name of the Game: 7 Indications I'd Be A Queer Flexitarian
Hadrian Shawn Miguel

<u>At This Stage of The Game</u>
7 kids, boys, brothers, amigos, homies, hermanos always ready
To jump, run, swim. laughing, looking, exploring
Navigating skate parks, playing kick ball, hot wheels & handball
                Keeps me from boredom & disdain

<u>The Name of the Game</u>
With my sisters, cousins, frienemigas, playing twister, show & tell, operation, doctor
Shooting toy guns, polaroids, and frosting with easy bake ovens
Shouting say say o' play mate & and you sank my battleship!
                My silly domain

<u>Fun and Games</u>
Escaping to the worlds of super mario bros, ms. pacman and donkey kong
Eating breakfast pancakes with bacon and pop tarts
Bag lunches of salame sandwiches with fruit cups, and cheese sticks
Afterschool candy stores, videos, tv, and dress-up
                I'm not ashamed

<u>Fair Game</u>
Before bedtime, the stories & showers, child's play with bubble baths
When they ate me out before I was 7
Boys will be boys with their toys
Their silly pissing contests, playing with fire
I liked it and didn't get burned
                No one is to blame

New Ball Game

The sport changed for me at 7
I wrote on the walls with lipstick
Then turned to look in the mirror with painted lips
I had to learn how to fight and moonwalk
                In the fire and rain

He Got Game

I was happy, fearless, and self aware
Clipper shaved my head and breakdanced
I perfected the backflip and splits
I played deejay and MC
                Kid glory and fame

Ahead of The Game

I helped cook my first vegetarian pasta dish
I saw Prince in stilettos, panties, and trench coat
I wrote some stories and rode in low riders
I sang falsetto with black nails
              I knew was queer
              In these words I proclaim

mi corazón de melón
Angel

You taught me that love is not always romantic
Love does not equal stress or pain
Love can come from someone you aren't fucking

You gave me bitter mezcal while I was trying to forget about what happened to me in December

You listened to me cry for over an hour while I had a panic attack because I was afraid of flunking out my second semester in college and because the boy I liked had hurt me once again.
I said, "I'm sad" over and over again because I didn't know what else to say.
You made me feel safe even though you were 3,000 miles away.

I came crying to your apartment with my broken heart for the billionth time
You played Solange in the background and put savila in my hair with your gentle hands.

I called you after picking up my books from the boy who had them for two years and never read them
I couldn't breathe and I felt like I was going to collapse
I felt stuck
I went to your home

You held me and told me you loved me very much
This is one of the few times someone told me this and I truly believed it

Cool Breeze
Hadrian Shawn Miguel

Timing is the key, a September song with a latch
As a door pushes forward, to open
Something's holding me back
I should step in, dive in feet first and not look

And what stirs the wind that now rushes on by
As I turn to face the air that's electrifying and unknown
The color of longing becomes
Two words, could've been

I never knew the breeze blowing by
Could've been you
I only knew when I first saw you
That my hands were tied to someone else
And at this deep hour of dusk
The rather tender sweet gust of air
Wouldn't let time upstage and interfere
With the cool breeze that is here

The reports came in that you adored my own gusty winds
Not just chasing another tumbleweed rolling by in the heat
But a dazzling wildflower growing through the concrete
I didn't know what to do next on this arid desert street

T i m e   d o e s n ' t   s t a n d s t i l l

A dry warm air now passes me by
As the palm of my hand is heavy with sweat
Then shifts, revealing a refreshing draft passing through
The cool breeze of Dr Feelgood *could've been* you

This River Flows
Hadrian Shawn Miguel

From atop the mountain high enough
Feel the motion growing
The crisp air has now become the heat
And the mighty river floweth between my legs and down my cheek

The mighty stream becomes a creek
An ocean of love and desire, I long to take a sip
I love to stick and dip my toes on the other side of the pond
This river knows

Like honey so sweet, the valley and meadows flooded
I feel the funk drizzling to my feet
The river overflows never missing a beat
The cream of the crop to see
Your salty ocean conducts my electricity
It runneth over somewhere between a minute and a lifetime
It's a fine line every time I get caught up in the surge

This river flows
Along my spine, through the valleys of my mind
Entrenched between my lips when they are wet
A steady movement is set
Rippling deep within in my heart
This river flows along my spine, on my face
On top my chest, down the small of my back
Drizzling on my thighs, penetrating the crack
Dark berry, sweet cherry, sometimes grapes of wrath
Along the river's edge, a rubyfruit jungle
Of savory figs, juicy plums and ripe bananas
To illuminate the rushing river path

You only ever want me when the light's out
Now I'm thrust in the dark
Sometimes I can only see you from the waist down

I know that you can only yearn for me when I lay down
A flood bursting at my core, this river rushes more & more
In the dead of night & the heat of day when others are not around

This river gushes deep and mountain high
Along my bayou inside the stormy lake
Within my high seas at my deep blue

This river flows along you, with me, on you
You watch as I roll round and round
When I come tumbling down the river
Listen to the sound of waters breaking and crashing
When this river flows

Cuando sale el sol
Yessica Avila

¡Ay mujer!

El sabor de tus labios, a un sueño me despiertan
todas la mañanas, como agua de piña fresca me refrescan
El mar verde azul de tus ojos, a mi alma gemela refleja
y desnuda, destrozando toda mi armadura

Cuando los dolores de la vida a mi a piel morena queman
las montañas de tus pechos, me asombran y cobijan
de la niebla que causa todas mis tristezas

Mientras las curvas de tu cuerpo, fielmente me navegan
A un mundo donde nunca se conoce la vergüenza,
Directo al punto entre tu piernas

—el cielo

¡Ay amorcito corazón!

More Bounce To The Ounce
Hadrian Shawn Miguel

midnight lady, Nars bronze you are
shimmering through, seeing you there

in the morning dew with foggy skies
strut, move, shake it mama, prance

boogie the house down, work it
lush syncopated rhythms, yes

beating congas light the fire,
full gyrating hips, fancy footwork

so fluid, we bachata in unison
trying not to stop but watch you

go into a trance, wittingly
spinning like a record, right round

looking forward, I fall into
potholes, my stiletto breaks in two

mad skills, electrifying, lit
bodies twist, shift, spin, dip, pose

my eye's still on the prize, you sway
rock steady, more bounce to the ounce

Food Porn
Hadrian Shawn Miguel

When I look into your eyes
I see you jump out from the page of a magazine
Your photo is amazing
The dew of your glistening skin
You are all avocado oiled up
I want to share all of you on social media
I see you moved all your Tumblr to Twitter
A nice, tight shot on my screen
My mouth waters in bliss and anticipation
I swallow and wet my lips

When I see you at the store
An assortment and bursts of textures and colors
Arranged in such a special way
To make me want you even more
Than when I saw you the last time
So ambrosial my mind explodes

When we go out to dinner,
You are savory & sweet
You smell soooooooo effin' good
I couldn't resist your sweat and aroma
So salty, honeyed and smoked
When I taste and take a bite
The bittersweet bang of a cooking delight
Nothing but a luscious lemon to break up all the fat
Of your slim jim bacon bits on a hot tuna melt

I relish your cherries and screeches
So succulent and fulfilling
Peeled bananas, and green plaintains
Sprinkled with sofrito and azafrán
You tickle my fancy
Those eggplants, okra, melons
Pickled cucumbers and prickly pears so juicy

Tantalizing
I want to squash you all up
In cashew butter and cream
And eat you all the way up
Drip by drip and bite by bite
You satisfy all my food porn
And joys of sex

Maria
Yessica Avila

Soft,
thick,
sharp,
Brown,
Skin
12:50
"ding dong, ding dong,"
the church bell rings
Purple orange skies,
Timid warm breeze,
summer is here
You stand there,
"Jefe de Jefes"
Head up high,
branching out of the rusted bars
they've
tried,
But
they
Could not
Scars of the
memories
The burning pain
you know so well
they've tried,
But they
Could not
stop the
tender,
soft,
pink,
Yellow,
daffodil and gilli f l o w e r s   g r o w i n g   a t   y o ur   f e e t

The Bed Left Undone
Hadrian Shawn Miguel

From the stairs of your house
Looking out I could see
The streets of desire
Lined with plumeria trees
Your great big temple of joy
So caramel, so chocolate, so alabaster-
So him, so her, so them I enjoy.

From the street
Gazing in I dreamt of the kiss
Those arms wrapped around so tight
The light is bright and warm
Always tempting as I dance in the storm
In the home your lips so soft & wet
Inviting me always into your charm

Your house like your body
Feels sleek and strong
It hides walls of darkness
At times I belong

If you open the door and take a peek
Into a mind seriously beaten
And fingers badly broken
In the open window I speak a fire
So burning, I choke.
And a fist, my dear friend
The sharp tongue twisted to the end

All the exchanges
And you cast the first of many stones
My words don't compare
My words get stuck in my throat

Reciprocation is lonesome
When love is just not deep between your knees
I close my eyes
I no longer see

The damage is done
The bed will never be the same
Broken on both sides
Dislocated and spun

And, what is worse?
The words or the stroke
The window's more revealing
To the voices on the street
My hands are all shaking
My voice is played out
As I wake up on the couch

This is not ideal
Simply, not right
The words you can't undo
And, the fist's another issue
Has anyone really won?
With the house in disarray
When the bed is left undone

CROSS✞ROADS
Hadrian Shawn Miguel

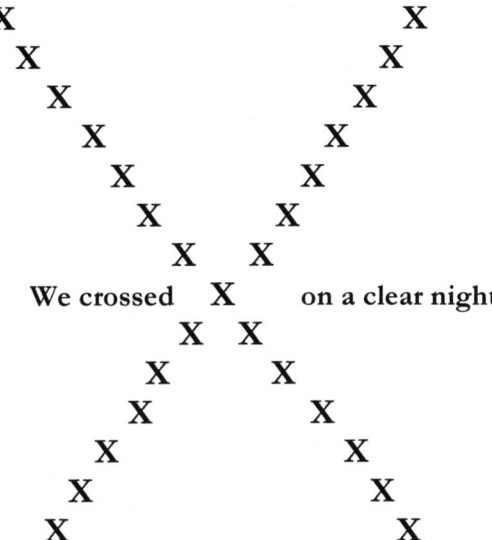

We crossed X on a clear night

The road paved deep
Leading down a garden path
The ride fast & steep

Then a sudden turn ↵

And you were there still looking around
Trailing in the back searching in every which way
For carnal desire from someone else long gone

I swiveled right ➔

You stayed ⊙ here
stunted
Unable to rise above & move forward

I jumped over a black rainbow
And found my liquid gold

Here I stand + alone
Newfound bliss

Take the s out of sex, you're just an ex
Take the l out of lover, and it's over
x o x o
Just exes + oh's
I hear you panting from behind

Wash Cycles on Learning How to Forget a Lesbian Womanizer
Lorilyn Luong

Delicates
Lather lavender lotion onto your skin
to repel her away
Realize the bite turned into an infection
and the infection into invalidation
every time
she left and returned
and said bisexuality doesn't exist

Rinse and Spin
Load the washer with heavy fabric
from her father's vomit of daily demeaning
and her mother's silence folded down as tradition
Air-dry the laundry that couldn't speak the family's dirty
Find socks with holes
from summer days walking with her,
and throw them away
Donate the faded red jacket she gave you when you were cold
Bleach the lipstick stains from the grandfather, who taught the
father, who taught the sons
who love women
that It's all about how many
girls you can get wet.
Smell the new scent, so that
you don't see her when she's not there anymore

Speed Wash
Distract yourself
Soak your heart in lukewarm water, boil the leash she holds to
try to forget
Delete the new friend requests she sends
To not mess up the forwarding motion

Permanent Press
Crack your spinal cord straight
Do not slouch down to glittery wrappings when the present does not contain
Change

Normal
Begin to find yourself after losing yourself
by not giving any more chances
Adjust settings to default to remember why
this is the last time
and there will be no more chances

Cleaning to do list:
☒Her

Progressions

Entwendent: [ehn-**twen**-dent]
Lauren Feller

adjective

Somewhere between total integration into someone else's life and a physical dependency on their existence in yours. The way it feels when you take a shower together, or share the same side of a table during your second date. When over half of your weekly wardrobe comes from their closet, and your playlist is made up of a genre of music you never bothered to listen to before. The thoughtless way you pick a piece of dandruff out of their hair, the added weight on your keychain, the spot at the foot of your bed where your dog had curled up at their feet every night, even though they hated the extra heat. The laundry they would bring over every Sunday, using the machine in your kitchen more than you did. The apricot sparkling water you kept your fridge stocked with, because it was their favorite

The unthinkable, unbearable space   that forms in their absence

the missing
Lauren Feller

it's the strangest thing —
i miss peeing with you
sharing a bathroom stall, however small
i miss the simple, quiet, silly intimacy
(our seeping, creeping, codependency)
i miss your impossibly small bladder
& the way it would constantly
inconvenience me
i miss the way you wasted rolls of toilet paper,
gallons of water,
bottles of soap,
you could never feel fully clean

it's the hardest thing —
i miss being with you,
between broken glass, my shattered sanity
and sobs so loud they scared the dog,
i miss
the days
the nights
the morning
the fights
that came with that all-consuming, impossible
task of loving someone
who wasn't ready to love me.

soiled
Lauren Feller

what's been seen
can't be unseen —
so i still can't sleep on
your
side of the bed.

what has been lost, sometimes,
(rarely)
can be found again,
but we've already tried that, haven't we,
two years, too many
attempts to get it right
only to end up
back   here.

what is shrouded in darkness
will once more be illuminated —
but you left in the dead of night and i'm still waiting
for the sun to rise.

what is watered will bloom,
what is not, will wither and die,
(But no matter how many weeds i let grow)
i cannot seem to kill you.

a dialectic
Lauren Feller

what i want ──────── what i want to want

I want her back
I want to hold her again, smell her
& her skin, touch her hand under tables
to touch her in places I no longer touch
myself

I want to let her go
I want to wake up without the aches
I want the blackhole that tore open
to seal itself shut & save me from
myself

I want to apologize for everything I did wrong
(and for some things I didn't)
I want to make her feel
~~I want to feel~~
loved again

I want to forgive myself
for becoming so lost—for throwing myself
under the same bus, over and over,
like roadkill.
I want to believe I will be
loved again

I want to wear
her thoughts, feelings,
underwear, dresses,
one last time —
just to see if they still fit,

or if they

I want to believe I can find
the good parts again someday
without the harm, the chaos,
the conditioning.

I want to believe in myself more than
she

ever could.

Love Poem for a Friendship That Feels Like Freedom, And Therefore Teaches Me How To Be More Myself
Audrey Kuo

can't beat the blissful joy
of hanging with my summer boys
bodies free of cis concern
moving quick toward yearning,
skin on skin
this blessing sinful, simple
so cute and so sweet, your soft lips
my summer treat
front stoop kisses
tender bliss is
these moments we exist
and see love as resistance
my summer femme
my sweet they/them
until next time,
when we meet again

We Laugh and Prance
Audrey Kuo

I cherish this, the sweetest joy
bodies flowing, feeling free
just hanging with my summer boys
our love a mirror reflecting, we

bodies flowing, feeling free
I learn to move aligned with spirit
our love a mirror reflecting, we
sing our own praise, lean in to hear it

I learn to move aligned with spirit
with every step we float, we dance
sing our own praise, lean in to hear it
we bend, we dip, we laugh and prance

with every step we float, we dance
we come alive, return to home
we bend, we dip, we laugh and prance
aligned, complete, our bodies our own

we come alive, return to home
prepare our souls for easy bliss
aligned, complete, our bodies our own
alive in the moment of sweet first kiss

what our gender is: freedom
Audrey Kuo

boys who touch, who dance
whose clothes smell of sunshine, sweat
boys who are not boys

Writing
J. Daniel Cruz

I write for my own freedom
I write to talk alone
I write to tell the world of the horrors that I've known.

I write to know myself
I write to not forget
I write to bind on paper the demons that torment my days

I write to keep on living
I write to talk to the unborn
I write to stay forever with the ones that I love.

A Place in your Heart
J. Daniel Cruz

After all the time we have spent
After the smiles, caresses and soft words left unsaid
I hoped I'd earned a place in your heart
In fairness from when you took mine

But I see I'm nowhere near
I'm just a pastime you take twice a year
I'm someone whose name you wouldn't say
I'm the fool who loves you from the very first day

What is left for me to do?
How do I erase your touch?
How do I carve it away?
How do I forget?

I had hoped I earned a place in your heart
After all, you settled down in my soul
Harvested, took, exploited
Leaving me homeless in my own body

Hummingbird
J. Daniel Cruz

Hummingbird of rainbow colored wings
Moving swiftly to the beating of my heart
For you have traveled from seas to hills
Leaving many in the trail of your charm

Among the foxgloves, among jasmines
Sampling honey from sugary lips
Glide and twirl, seduction your wings inspire
A lonely rose whose nectar your desire

My love, my admiration no one hurt
Your beauty I'd never hoped to contain
Yet you plagued my soul in form of flirt
Engulfed me in a world of pain I'd never complain

Escape again into the dark
Away from their judgy glance
The way we did many a night
Under the cold moonlight
A hungry kiss, A desperate grasp
A way to pay a secret romance
Let it burn, let it scar, let it rasp
Under your touch of cruel delight

The tears are good they water the ground
Decaying petals that have fallen down
From ashes moistened of my own grievance
Bloom again, love again I shall, despite inconvenience

A Rose is Always a Rose
J. Daniel Cruz

A rose is always a rose
A thorn accompanies a feeling
It pricks when you grasp
It stabs when you hold on to it

To love a rose is to endure the pain
Remember the scars it left during May

But I don't want to love and suffer

If you loved me you wouldn't hurt me
If I loved you I'd let you bloom
If loving you makes me bleed
And by gripping you I damage you

Let us let go of each other
Let us heal from one another

A rose is always a rose
But to love it
It is not necessary to hold it.

Remember
J. Daniel. Cruz

Every single day I pray
Of things I hope soon forget
But the time I spent at your side
The feel of your heartbeat and mine
Will never leave my mind
Till the day I die

The smiles I smiled
The lips I kissed

Spark long forgotten that burns within
Alive in my heart will always be
Till again I see you smiling at me

I hope one day I will
As hope itself extinguished will be
More than anything left there is
I'll hope you remember me still

Missing You
J. Daniel Cruz

I miss the way you smell

The way you desperately take me without care
The way I kissed you before sunrise
Because in your slumber you knew not
That I caressed you like the Greeks worship the sun

When I woke and I bestowed
Your beauty
I cradled your soul
Your body
Beyond what is understood

And I miss you

Like the flowers miss the morning dew
Without you I feel like I wither

Slowly
Agonizing

But I know that you could never feel what I feel for you
It is my tragedy that encapsulates me into my own tomb

Still I miss you like the desserts miss the rain

Like the moon misses the sun
Resignation that stings with unendurable pain

And I live in despair

If only you could have a hint of feeling
That for your affections
I would cross Hades without inhibitions

If by tradition, yearning you deems me unholy
    Let them sizzle my flesh into a crisp
Filling my heart with memories of melancholy
    Lover, with your kiss I can die in bliss

Thoughts and Prayers
J. Daniel Cruz

Do not say sorry now.
About the horrors you've allowed

Your thoughts and prayers won't make a difference
When there was a time to speak for the innocent
You made a statement with your blatant ignorance

Do not say you are sorry
When in a rightful rage they screamed "Black lives matter'
You shot back "No, all lives matter"

Do not say you are sorry
When the cries of refugees blasted in the air
You screamed fake news and looked the other way

When children were kept without food or water
You said should know better before crossing a border

When women were assaulted left and right
You called them whores. Boys will be boys and left it at that

Do you even like yourself?

What will you do when there is no one left to destroy?
Look into a mirror and slay yourself with your own sword?

Carry your shame for generations to come
In your conscience like chains forged in stone
Maybe then you won't forget how you forgot
The horrors of a world war

But how can you presume to know our frustrations?
When your self-preservation
Has led to the destruction of other nations

The things I would say to the kid in the frame
J. Daniel Cruz

1- You're going to be all right.
2- You will grow up. You will know love.
3- The pain and suffering though bleak will not break. The scars made time will erase.
4- It isn't a choice. You can't change. You can't pray it away.
5- Don't let their hurtful words define you. Only you can define you.
6- You are loved. I wish you heard that more.
7- Your life is precious. Please don't try to cut it short
8- It will get better.
9- You were meant to fall in love. Your story won't end with tears and hurt.
10- They will judge and reject you. It isn't your fault.
11- Family are those who love you unconditionally. Blood is got nothing to do with it.
12- Whatever the future holds. We are gonna be all right.

FUCK
Andrea-Celeste Jimenez

In the 3 a.m. silence, your whisper is the only thing keeping me up

"I'm gonna fuck you"

But all I hear is:

                fuck the shit out of you

                    fuck your brains out

                      fuck up your life

I'm saying fuck, I gotta get outta here before he fucks it up

fuck-FUCK

F U C K!

"Do you like me? I need to know"

He tries to kiss me but fucks it up

so as I leave…

He says wait

but I'm gone

you weren't trying to love me; you were just trying to fuck."

Home
Andrea-Celeste Jimenez

we're home late, getting back from the beach

twilight across the floor, creeping in

you're sitting away from me, drink in hand

what a good night it's been, to come home with you

the dogs are calm and the revel too

I can see the tv but I'm just watching you

RISE
Andrea-Celeste Jimenez

If I could rip myself to shreds

& give way to all anxiety
these waves of emotion out with ease
--breezing through the tilting tides of living a daily dying life
surrendering who I was yesterday; a meek, unseen, unheard, her?

Sighing out salty air of the tides
Squeezing juice from lemons
Rose gold tanning of the sun
plumerias breezing in the wind

Releasing. Restless. Rage.
Rising to be the sun and spreading warmth through light
Then becoming the moon, reflecting all the energy I set into motion
Resting, reliving and reinventing all of who I am

Someone deserving...

To rise again and again

Well?
Andrea-Celeste Jimenez

Where couldn't we be without each other, I held you in my heart, my hand, my head

like a lover.

You'd told me you wanted to be better, I believed you-I still believe you but you're nowhere

I sent the calls, messages, I know you feel it.

because remind me if I'm wrong there wasn't anyone who could break us

underneath our veil of all the years behind, no one but you knew better...

and so the devastation from our deforestation has brought disintegration atop our empty parking lot

offerings

it's not like you're spineless, I've felt you

What happened?

I wanted you; to have and to hold you

But what did you want?

In the midst you didn't even realize what it was we were, maybe you did?

But it hurt you so much to believe such a solid form of what you didn't let yourself see something that had never been a commodity, you made through rough eyes of pain, not yours

& I wonder

if you hadn't been so despairing with the distraction of another, would it have meant you really--

like you said bawling; crawling... so drunk and free'd reaching desperately, alone-one last time.

it was then I knew my attempts to show you what it meant weren't in vain

You just knew who you were, and for me?

I'll always carry what you saw from the beginning.

The end, you said:

"I can't love you the way you deserve to be loved"

Suspension with(out) suspense
Andrea-Celeste Jimenez

The wind on a damp face
sensations of comfort after the storm

`the suns heading up and you're still crying
I'm stunned by the words you had to wake me up for

And as long as I had been waiting to hear them,
I didn't want them-as much as I wanted...

just like the leftover cereal
that floats atop the milk

no one knows what to do with them anymore

A New Dictionary

Pascioon [pass-c-on]
Albus Wang

noun

Pascioon starts at the moment you realize your life is just a facade. It's a product from the assembly line made with false rules and limitations. You realize you are in a cage, safe but you have to be a certain shape to be in that cage. Then you find a small crack, a sign that the cage is not indestructible. You start to rethink everything you know, everything you think you know. Breaking the cage is never easy and struggle comes right after. They want to put you back to the cage and they threaten you with everything you have. Yet you do not look back because you see the world outside that is shining with all kinds of stars and you can be one of them. With all your power, you break out of the cage. In this new world, you start to build your life from the ground up. New wardrobe, new friends, new routine, new mind, and nothing is off the limit. You start from zero and everything you create is yours and only yours. Now you are ready to help others in the cage to see the world that is too good to be true. I had my pacisson, like a bungee jump off the cliff with an incomparable view. Pascioon is a grandulous, fabulous, and fantasticulous transformation combined with realization, struggle, and creation, about reevaluate, reimagine, rebirth, relive, and rebuild.

Cognitive Renaissance [kog-ni-tive ren-uh-sahns]
Lorilyn Luong

noun

It's the last challenge before the reward comes. Gauntlet in hand not swinging through the head of what was once considered enemy. It's the last grip let loose, removing the dried mud left over from stomping what was already made to be dead but was chosen to be kept alive instead. No applause from the audience, no medallion caressing the neck, no speaker bio before the stage entrance; all because of the feeling of what's right. You throttled rebellion in your veins, switched gears from follower to leader of your own. It's the deep sighs you let out when no one is around. Eyes making its way passed past trophies with your name, honoring a you, you once knew. Eyes staring back from a mirror reflecting the real you: Back. Alive. Mind postmarked to its original body. Destination: To return to self, *Synonyms: Self-remembrance*

Postrastir [pos trae ster]
librecht baker

verb

1. A being continuously possessed by time and constraints of time designated by a bleached trust in linear, successive occurrences while, however, feeling, speaking, and wearing a wool coat of all time -past, present, and forthcomings - at once, & simultaneously changing present while being future now; the mannerism in which time engages its position of influence; a thing concurrently once is and never was; a dimensional truth & falsified visceral existence; a restricted, unstrict machine.

2. A human being whose body is mounted by a spirit traveling between realms and/or dimensions, i.e Egun, Oshun, Yemoja, etc. *synonyms: mounted, possession, holy ghost, presence of oludumare's angelic forces, a love supreme, racing heart, African spirit; sound mind, holy spirit, bliss, earth-based spirituality, the future now, right now etc.*

3. Possessed travel; possession of a traveling spirit humanized.

nown

you, the person reading this text, as a reflection of your lineage, i.e. past, present, and forthcoming; people.

*Definition stirred by *Black Quantum Futurism: Theory & Practice* (The Afrofuturist Affair, 2015) and other happenings.

Ricannected [ree–kăn–nek–tid]
Hadrian Shawn Miguel

verb

Of or related to being united, joined, or linked by intersectionalizations, interwoven & interconnected from upheavals of a soiled past. The roots of this tree are homespun from seeds bloodied from the colonization of Spain into the Caribbean intermixing with European settlers, exploitations of Taíno indians & African slaves, no longer running free. The fertile ground on which I stand was also planted & seasoned with an adobo spice, tainted too, and known as the islands named in honor of King Philip. Rape, executions, cross pollinations, extinctions, causations forcing us to coexist, fellations, fornications, emasculations, ablations, ramifications, fortifications, translations, dictations, placations, castrations, objectifications, infiltrations, the vast limitations, condemnation, vilifications, experimentations, violations, criminalization, contamination, and corruption in the history of the Puertorriqueño & Filipino people. No recantations, reparations, retributions, restitution or atonement are jointly needed. We are ricannected by migrations and mutations of who we are that cannot or will not be undone.

Pre(judice) & Healing

Albus Wang

Boxes, boxes, boxes, boxes; Where is we should be
Boxes, boxes, boxes; Hearing them all, seeing them all

Boxes, boxes; I stare at the abyss
Boxes; Only thing stayed now

Hands waved, engine on; See the back disappear
Hugs gave, tears down; Sit with the vain strike near

Boxes are our lives

Boxes; memories, lives, belongings, belongingness
Boxes, boxes; stacked up in the living/room

Boxes, boxes, boxes; come and leave, here and gone
Boxes, boxes, boxes; nowhere to go, nowhere to stay

Don't leave, my friend; I couldn't say
For the sake of our future; Along our past

Glass clinked, words out; Wishing you all the goodness
Air swirled, laughs pass; Wishing you all the nicest

States of Disgrace
Hadrian Shawn Miguel

In a broken world of tweets and #hashtags
Abbreviations & improper English
Texts instead of phone calls
Straight to sex on dating apps instead of dinner & drinks
Or not even coffee or tea for that matter
Shorthand languages in a mobile world
A swipe up or to the left instead of pages from a book turned
The laziness of idk and lmk
LOL's and IDGAF
The demise of western civilization…and tumblr
When social media and emojis are king

This land was their land
With native voices chanting, sacred & unscorned
Multiple centuries old, way long before you & I
#Native #Indigenous
Stupid Twitter feeds
#45 #STFU
Rampant mumbles and utterings
Racism, white nationalism, domestic terrorism
Threats, mass shootings, massacres, gun violence
Are all building a greater divide
A constant state of beating down & killing Blacks
ICE-ing up with detention centers & deporting Browns
#Inhumanity #Indignation #Injustice
Why migrant detention centers remind us of an awful part in history
#InternmentCamps
I need a #TBT for the type of man that was JFK or MLK
Keeping 💯

Sexual harassments and even more beat downs
#MeToo
Raping and killing Queens of all kinds
Not a time for a selfie or a meme
I am PROUD with #Pride
But not proud to be in this current united states of disgrace
No more this land was made for you and me

20/20 vision, I see you
#2020
All the brilliant colors of a charcoal & muddy rainbow
Building bridges instead not walls
And karate kick the Orange out
Will #civilunrest lead to
Jubilation like when the Berlin wall came tumbling down
#RiseUp 🙏

lucky number: 1992
librecht baker

1992, some Black voters, 10.55% of LA's population, rebelled post-verdict,
schoolers learned adjudication's emerge,
and others accepted worse
was adjacent. or, our amassed vexation and grief seen
was televised. darker complexions, only rebels broadcast while
i perched first row in miss bigot's science class.

1992, miss xenophobe sported knee-jean skirts in class
seated with a post-verdict
retched flat faces while
traversing right ankle over left knee, her thigh emerged
divulging intimacies seen,
but her anti-Black foible was worse.

1992, i vacationed elsewhere of worse
buttress with family from science class.
long beach boulevard and 20th, the unrest wasn't seen.
we recessed for seven days post-verdict.
while businesses burned, we emerged
ahead of racism's exhausted sulfuric burnt funk, beyond a while.

1992, returning to hill middle school, miss white-flight leered at me while
saying, *you had no reason to miss school,* and worse
her bitter lip emerged
encumbered with pre-post-verdict
beliefs and intolerant vernacular in class.
my Mother made our magnificence seen.

1992, my Mother revivified our Blackness. we were seen.
administrators paid anti-Black educators while
miss illiberal revered salutations made of pre-post-verdict

and discussed orca dick. worse
i was in science class
learning how Blackness is duressed, yet emerges.

1992, we emerge
my family guarded our seen
while untutored teachers instructed racially in class
with indications i'd be Black-american while
worse
a not guilty typhoon spiraled us counterclockwise post-verdict

in 1992, bulbous charcoal clouds emerged while harrowing post-verdict
citizens are continuously seen in 2019, and worse a barbarous blue badged class revels its repast while egalitarianism gobbles bones.

Every night before I sleep
Yessica Avila

La luna y las estrellas whisper in my ear,
        A Stubborn Taurus akin to you,
       never welcome change

But if a shooting star
    could grant me a wish....
....Just one wish
    I would ask to please,
        Rewrite my yesterdays
  Bc
If I could,
    I would change a couple things

        No more hasta luegos
        Que el viento desaparece
        No more innocence lost
        en el fuego del desierto
        No more lágrimas de sangre
        born in the unknown
If I could,
    I would change a couple things

        No more noches solitarias
        sin querer tener un sueño
        No more stumbling in
        two languages
        Mah na
            mmmm
              ....ees
                  /Meeeee
                Nom
                        brrrrrrrr-be
                        Is

                No more sharp, sinking, pain
                When they shout la migra

    If I could,

            I would change a couple things
                No more calling us wet bags
                No more losing our humanity
                        No more American Dream

like the white kids
Angel

Growing up I hated being brown
Never looking up
Always looking down

I wish I could dream
like the white kids
Given the entire earth since birth
Controlling every single thing in the world
Black and brown kids losing spots in colleges to some boring dude named Chad
Can't believe someone asked me why I'm so fucking mad
We're losing everything
To gentrification
Black and brown kids feeling stuck no matter their dedication

I wish I could have fun
like the white kids
Carefree at the frat parties
Economic hierarchy shown through the frat house bids

The lord is testing me
This white girl spilled her drink on me
She laughs and pretends she can dance
I bet she's only here cuz her dad does finance

In class some stupid white dude says something racist
I call him out but this dude can't face it
He's an asshole but everyone thinks I'm the jerk

I had to overshare my traumas to get into Berk
I have to share about my homies in jail, in the streets, just to prove that I can get this career
The people giving me money feed off my fear

"I'm a brown poor person, and
oh shit yeah
I'm queer"

Letter to the oppressed, from an oppressed
Yessica Avila

Blind they choose to be,
selective memory
ignoring
        all that is Bloody.

a facade of dreams

        w h i t e
                blanket,

Maliciously,
consuming all
that can exist,
leaving
only the Hurt,
the Tears

Abyss of
        w h i t e
                nesssss,

lurking for the last
Warm breath of Hope
to infiltrate
Souls
relatively
close to their pale
        w h i t e
skin and
slowly spread
        w h i t e   s u p r e m a c y
through our blood streams

Remember...
The time you called her puta,

shamed her femininity,
convicted her body,
And question her morality?

      w h i t e
            nesssss

The day you ignored her words
And refused to see a
real woman bc she had no
pussy?
      w h i t e
            nesssss

When like a fatal weapon
you used science and
religion to erase all that
is non-binary

      w h i t e
            nesssss

Do you recall?
When you said viva la raza,
The reborn Aztlan,
Cafe con leche,
the new supreme

      w h i t e
            nesssss
Bc
You my dear oppressed,
are an oppressor even
if it's not clear to see

They are Not Here
Albus Wang

This is the moment I feel living alone is hard.

I have my	support system.
I have my	intimate confidants.
I have my	chosen family.
But I am	the only one here.

Technology helps me talk to them.
Technology helps me listen to them.
But technology can't help me.
touch them.
So ar away.

People who can understand	me
are not	here.
People who can	hug me
are not	here.
People who can	pat me
are not	here.

People who bully me
are not here.
They don't understand
what I have been
and what I am going through.
They assume I live in the
same world.
They are not here.

They can wreck	my home.
They can wreck	my mind.
They can wreck	my soul.
They are not	here.

They don't sense		the damp.
They don't sense		the moist.
They don't sense		the ocean.
They are not		here.

They don't sniff		the sniff.
They don't smell		the smell.
They don't disgust		the disgust.
They are not		here.

They don't see		the crawling.
They don't see		the hanging.
They don't see		the holding.
They are not		here.

The text message		is here.
The email		is here.
The letter		is here.
They		are not here.

The blame they sent		is here.
The shame they sent		is here.
The defame they sent		is here.
They		are not here.

They don't ask if I		sleep well at night.
They don't ask if I		sleep at night.
They don't ask if I		sleep.
They		are not here.

It's just a phone call.		That's what they said.
We are all adults.		That's what they said.
I'm sure we are		adults.
Because adults		assume.
Because adults		hurt.
Because adults		murder.

There goes   the apology
I thought   was there.
No.
I checked   again.
I checked   another time.
I checked   one last time.
I find   no apology.

Misfortune,   maybe.
Time difference,   maybe.
Miscommunication,   maybe.
Disrespect,   must be.

They have   big words.
They have   big attitudes.
They have   big rhetoric.
I could only   bow and kneel.

Right, I am   no victim.
I need   no apology.
I am   the problem.
That's   what they said.
They   are not here.

I ask you to   look at that wall.
Don't you see?   The wall is wet.
I ask you to   look at the floor.
Don't you see?   The floor is wet.
I ask you to   look at the wood.
Don't you see?   The wood is wet.
They are not   here.

I ask you to   touch my slippers.
Can't you feel?   My slippers are wet.
I ask you to   touch my feet.
Can't you feel?   My feet are wet.
I ask you to   touch my bedding.
Can't you feel?   My bedding is wet.

They are not   here.

It's the email   with heading.
It's the letter   with heading.
It's the card   with heading.
Under the   shadow
I can only   see their shoes.
They are   not here.

They are gonna paint over   the wood.
They are gonna paint over   the wall.
They are gonna paint over   the heart.

But the wood cannot just be   painted over.
But the wall cannot just be   painted over.
But the heart cannot just be   painted over.

I won't let them just   paint over.
I won't let them just   cover up.
I won't let them just   live through.

My wall   needs to be healed.
My home   needs to be healed.
My heart   needs to be healed.
There is   one single way.

In the script they gave me,
I am   the antagonist.
I am   the evil.
I am   the villain.

They are   not wrong.
I will be   the antagonist.
I must be   the evil.
I am being   the villain.

indications that i'd be a sad bitch
Angel

At age 7 I tried killing myself for the first time
I cried in the kitchen with a knife to my stomach
I didn't understand why my life was so shitty
I thought the way I lived was my fault
No love, in poverty, and alone
I didn't kill myself then, but I've thought of doing it ever since

At age 11 I started isolating myself
I didn't want to see or talk to anyone at all
I'd hide behind my stupid emo hair
I wanted to hurt myself

At age 14 it was difficult to even go outside
I felt too much at the same time
I was angry, miserable, anxious, and numb
I'd get home from school and hide in my room
I'd sleep at 6 pm because
I didn't want to feel anymore

At age 18 my world was changing and endless opportunities
were coming my way
I didn't think I would have made it this far
I had a bright future
I had been accepted to a top school with everything paid for
I was going to live far away and have a fresh start
I tried to not let all the sadness I felt consume every bit of
progress I made

I still wanted to die
But I also wanted to want
to live so bad

alcoholismo zapoteco
Angel

I remember listening to the fast words escaping from my tio's
and tia's mouths at family gatherings in a small apartment on 8th
I never knew what the words meant
But I knew they felt like home

I remember playing with my cousins till dark
When the fast words began to *slur*
Dozens of empty Coronas across the floor

Waking up the next morning to
An empty bottle of rubbing alcohol next to my primo's hand
Tios, primos, and my abuelito passed out on the carpet
/
I'm on my 12th shot of vodka
Being drunk isn't as fun anymore
I used to dance for hours
Laughing
In dark rooms with bright lights and loud radio music

Now I'm in my friend's room on a school night
She's sober and listening to me rant about not being good enough
About my fears

"I'm killing myself today."

I don't remember what she replies
I don't remember how I got home
I wake up the next day wishing I hadn't

things i wish i could've told you instead of pretending i forgave you
Angel

Stop calling me an indian
Shut the fuck up
Stop comparing me to your white girlfriend
I'm sorry she's boring but
Don't tell me you like me
Get off me
Don't tell me you were having a good time
and I ruined it because I was too drunk to function and kept falling over
Stop trying to contact me every few months to apologize
I won't forgive you
Leave me alone

Alive
Lorilyn Luong

                                                     The self is becoming
                                                   When body's not numbing
                                                        Mind's not loathing
                                                           Yang and ying
                                                           Start to swing
                                                           Laugh and sing
                                             To what's been missing
                                                           In this healing
                                             After the mourning
                                         Felt by this wing
                                     That stings, this tearing
                                     Finding its motion
                           Amongst all the commotion
                           Soft words become lotion
                             Flight is the potion
                  After what's been broken
                    It is time to be open
                    Flood all the oceans
Words finally spoken
I am golden
And I have awoken

Touch
Albus Wang

touch me, touch me
the tree said
i need love
the tree said

i felt it
i felt the tree

i felt its rough skin
i touched its weathered texture outside
the tree needs my love
or just anyone's love

the tree is warm
comparing to its friends
it is warm
because some trees are cold
go touch them
trees have their own temperature

this tree must like me
it's inviting me to touch it
unlike other trees
told me to go away
they said *enough*
when I touched them
but this tree gave me warmth
this tree gave me hope

it looks so small
it looks so experienced
it looks so strong
i thought
with support
it tries to survive
it tries to grow

i felt its hairy leaf
i observed its crossed veins
i didn't know leaf could be hairy
like the cheek of my face
like someone's ear back

between the leaves
small fluffy balls are budding
they shout out vitality

yes the balls are fluffy
because of the tiny hair on them don't
laugh at the balls
they look like my balls
your balls
her balls
his balls
their balls
so don't laugh at the balls
they are thriving

bees are beaming
dancing through the branches
flying through the leaves
bzzzz
bzzzz
it's a reminder
to be careful
or else my left hand might be in danger

the breeze shakes the tree
the breeze shakes me
go with the wind
the tree said
i hold onto the trunk
we swing
with each other

Oh that hurts
i touched a thorn
except it's not a thorn
but the broken part of the branch
which is sharp and pointy
it protects the tree
it's the evidence of pain

don't leave because of the scar
it's history
it's honor
it's celebration
i celebrate with the tree

touch me touch me
i need love
the tree didn't say
i did

fear of swallowing waves and plankton at cabrillo beach
librecht baker

1. Stand between the pier where fishers reel marine life upward swimming between states and
breakwater: ocean, winds, and, saltwater.

2. Descend rocks while disregarding marine isopods.

3. Be shoeless, hitch your denim jeans toward your knees, remove the brass-copper bracelet, and
tuck your Toyota Camry key somewhere by the rocks; remember which beachrock.

4. Deduce from your trepidation. Then, descend seabed as though it has fins.

5. Carry red, yellow, or orange hibiscus flowers and squash drizzled with rum forward to the
saltwater. What are you offering?

6. Pray a praise into the basket of hibiscus swinging your energy and lay them between oceanic legs
with a strong throw.

7. Touch water; descend rocks and allow watery fingers tickling. You cannot bestow gratitude from
there with ancestral Post Traumatic Slave Syndrome. Why remove your shoes, and climb the
boulders, again? The isopods will bite you because you're not listening. Come down already!

8. When aquatic arms sweep outward, remind yourself it's likely six feet even though you will only
swim three feet out. If the liquid is clear, don't look downward. If it's high tide muddy, pray.

9. Don't swim toward pacific bottlenose dolphins! You are not a delphinus delphis.

10. Open your eyes! Closing them doesn't perish your fear of your nose, mouth, throat, and lungs
being inundated with seawater.

11. Stop listening to olokun and yemoya's harp. They'll lure you outward if your eyelashes kiss.

12. Stay away from the jetty's jutting stones.

13. Wet your feet first. Why discard your high top, dusty, red chuck taylors if you're indifferent to
seafaring's cocoon?

14. Is the lifeguard on duty?

15. If they aren't, don't wade further than knee deep, which is three feet already.

16. Swim parallel to shore if waves undulate outward. Don't worry, they'll throw you back cyclically.

17. Keep your eyes open and come in!

18. Remember, you are not plankton, crabs, dolphins, etc., so don't inhale in their realm.

19. Come in, already!

20. Dip your body in the vortex, but don't gift yourself to their lullaby.

21. Stop thinking about your past life when you were part of the forced violent migration: bald of
hair, other-ethnic languaged, under 30, dumped into ocean between continent's wealthy ports; by
then sharks had learned ships circumnavigation of currents. You are not there. You are here in
2019!

sun-drunk squirrel OR Sometimes a Rose Garden Is Too Full of Metaphors for a Poet to Simply Enjoy a Sunday Afternoon
Audrey Kuo

springy grass, a lawn that calls
nature as a poetry prompt:
tickle-sharp edges, lush invitation
highlighter shag carpet tucked around
carefully curated rose bushes

a cliché of thorns encircles beauty
spikes and petals, these
splashes of color, reminders
of the earth's devastating creativity
ephemeral, everlasting

sun-drunk, I offer
a perfect prism of watermelon
to a curious squirrel
they chitter in glee, accept it greedily
and together we munch

on the first hint of summer
already infatuated with spring
this moment, a promise
to be present, and pay attention
to notice what is

an abundance of pleasure
overflowing like grief does

the expansion of our aliveness
shapes the chasms of our loss
stretching the vessels of ourselves
that we may always be growing
we feel more to feel more

later, I will wonder on
the implications of sharing with Jason
(the squirrel wouldn't leave,
was making a femme uncomfortable
– I gave him a man's name)

if familiarity might lead to demise
that they might put him down
we have conditioned ourselves to fear pleasure
how it might reshape us,
be taken away

No One Told Me Every Love Poem Was A Love Letter to My Future Self
Audrey Kuo

who told you you could only write about hope?
that every sad poem has to end on an uplifting note
that you can only offer a snapshot of your pain
never bury others beneath your longing
who told you that your anger is unspeakable
not nearly enough water left to put out all the burning
who told you that you don't get to weep in someone else's arms

who said that being a woman of color means you are always
cleaning up someone else's mess, and also your own
told you that you could only ever offer help
and never ever ask to receive it
that you don't get to be a sad trans boy, even though you're not
    actually a trans boy, except you might be a boy sometimes
    when you're hanging with your boys – but that's not what
    this poem is about

who said being a poet has to be laser-precise descriptions,
identities with fixed definitions
that you don't get to not decide

who told you you could only write about despair?
only get to be trans if and when you feel the cold poison of
    disgust coursing through your chest and down your arms
like dysphoria is a synonym for realness
like dysphoria is the only thing that makes your body your own
like dysphoria is the only kind of water that flows through you
that you don't exist unless you've been erased
until no one knows how to say your name
that being comfortable means you were never really here?

who taught you that you have to suffer to become
– and who have you passed that lesson on to?

starchild, poetry is not a litany of suffering
just like healing is not pretending
you've never tasted grief before
no one said you don't get to feel
no one said you only get to feel broken

your joy is your medicine
your tears are your medicine
this poem, your voice, this space is your medicine

no one asked you to make yourself easier to swallow
like you haven't lived long enough to know
you are never going to please everyone
but goddamn if you don't keep trying
wouldn't be a Pisces and a Chinese girl
if you didn't stake your hopes on someone else's heart

and I know you know
the more you stretch your water balloon heart to cradle the grief,
the more joy that heart can hold

that's the thing about fuck the binary:
you are never only one place

femme, you are the hope & possibility in your bones
the tender heartache that reminds you that we were born to feel
the topography of grief and remembrance
you are the belief that we will win
and the mourning when we don't

it is the memory of liberation coursing through your body
that makes the hard shit hit so heavy

my love, no one said you don't get to cry
no one said to wipe that smile off your lungs
not to sing about freedom every dance you get
no one told you not to laugh through your tears
no one told you not to write this poem

well, no. they did tell you not to write this poem
but your silence only protects them

and you
you and me,
we're not doing that self-censoring shit anymore

Heirlooms
Lorilyn Luong

I was told that my Lola had more bone on her than skin
Her fingers would curl to the white and black keys
music in the Philippines playing
louder than her
lungs choked by leftover radiating clouds,
the elegant moving of her fingers *l o u d e r*
than the bombs dropping \\// and roofs falling //\\
My Lolo gave warnings to families
Saying
Leave now
to still be alive
Before I was born my Lola gave me
Air
So I wouldn't breathe gas

Under the gray sky
My Lolo's back was forced to face Earth
Feet burned from cigarettes belonging to a Japanese soldier
How he had to battle our own, Asian, to claim American
His eyes avoiding the sun with skin blistering
arms tied to spikes, and standing
not possible
with the beatings by the rifle
My Lolo would never tell them
when they asked if he was a spy or guerilla
Nor to my family that he was in captivity
His letters unlocked in a dusty briefcase in the basement
He told the generation before me
to not touch what's locked
50 years of writing to request disability benefits inside this case
To be believed
To appeal
To keep fighting for what's right on native land and abroad

My Lolo gave me
Fire
So I would be able to take risks and challenge

My Papa turns off the stove and asks me if I ate
The table is ready with fried rice and fish
I know he used to starve
((Wrap up bodies that didn't make it and throw them in the sea))
You had to not make a sound on the small boat
not turn on the light in the dark so pirates also couldn't see
|And on land in Vietnam|
when the communists knock on your door
You be quiet,
pretend you're not there,
    and go   *get out,*   *the planes are here.*
In America, my Papa gave me
Light
So I could see my future

My Mama turns on the light
Uses a fake address with a different zip code so I would wake up
to go to the better school
She has a whole shelf of picture albums of a family not in war,
award certificates
in the U.S
My Mama tells me when I step out the door
Alisto. Be alert. Watch your surroundings.
My walk to the store of *ay ch ch* and stares by men
Reminds me of why
I am aware of their dangers
of status stripped from college degrees not recognized,
of a plane ride that dreams of what's better
of blind voyages
of water breaking and dancing
to build my DNA
My Mama gave me
Water
So I could breathe life

Meet Me At The Bodega
Hadrian Shawn Miguel

Meet me at the bodega, the one here
on W 230th, in the heart of the jungle, the hustle
the grit of the grand burrough that's the Bronx
The Great Big Apple's 1 0 4 6 3
Where it's always so good to see my Papi
Works from sunrise to sunset, dawn to dark,
And many times in the stark starry night
24/7 to make it right for us all
For la familia's American Dream.
Here I have seen, his visions mixed with tears
And the gleam of a better place in life
In the fierce Nuyorican footraces

Come on by get your after night out snacks
Some bagels & lox and cherry ice cream
You can see us from the elevated
Subway tracks, down from your 5 floor walk up
Or on the front stoop you'll find Mami there
In her daytime best, so grab good advice
With your icy cold drinks to wash it all
Down to chill & cool your hot balmy sweat

And our Felix the Great Cat will greet you
With a purr, or a sneer, or run you out
Because we don't like rats or gangs of guys
Who like to loiter, trying for a slice
Of this girl's oh so juicy peach pie
From my infamous sister the cashier,
With her tetas out, trying to get some
Extra cash for her lil' fledgling career

Here's where you'll hear her announce and declare
Oh yes my girls are always out to play
There's just no other way so meet me here
At the bodega, let's chat and hangout

In the back, behind the stacks of plantains
Grab a bottle of wine, crackers and cheese
Some of Ma's picadillo & pastelillos
I can do you no wrongs, buy a copy
My mixtape says Miss Ivy in Fendi,
So Gucci, La Ivy the Queen of the
Boogie down rock steady boogaloo crew
You can also escape and take a taste
of soda from The Island's Old Colony grape
Pick up a bag of ice, get a six pack
Your tummy's so tight I wanna take a bite
Of your Mofongo, warm in my oven.
I forever say Echa pa'lante
Meet me at the bodega and there you'll
Find my abuelita with some huevos
And a hen in the back room where she stands

Proudly with a goat, some eggs, and chanting
Sundrenched and weathered so sunny & warm
Take my hand she says, I am ready to
Cleanse you from your vida's colossal storm
I'll mash it up in the wooden pílon
Will you please join me in glory & praise
To the Orisha, in tough times we say,
La piña está agria, let me
Mix up some cascarilla and olmo
Lotions & potions for all that ails you

At my altar to Yemaya like yours
And your Papi's to Oshun, I invoke
And give thanks & praise to remove you from
The haze of muddy waters, a burning light
Mixing palm oil with liver I bathe you
In river water to cure and guide you
I always ask to watch over us
Especially you mi vida, mi Ivy, mi corazon
From bad energy and all that ails you

I call on our Ancestors, the spirits
Expel it and create a barrier
Between the living and mystical realms
With candles, some spells, myrrh and frankincense
Visions and smoke show you a greater path
Like a paloma to find harmony
And peace, not just sex, but love's happiness
The body a mighty temple keep it
Sacred and secret, not everybody
Should have, taste or take it so damn freely
Wear white sage from our store in a locket
On a chain around the neck it protects

Here it's professed many a smiling face
That greets you here today are blessed
Strong hands that work hard here our full hearts lie
Love in abundance our family resides
Meet me at the bodega day after day
Til the next time you come through we will say
Buenas noches and a loving goodbye.

Contributors:

Albus Wang (they/them) is a writer, an artist, and a recent graduate from Loyola Marymount University with a Theatre Arts bachelor's degree. Seeking social justice and overall equality, Wang is also an activist passionate about causes such as rights for immigrants and LGBTQ+ community. As a trans and non-binary writer, Wang works to empower trans community around the world by giving them a voice through literacy.

Andrea-Celeste Jimenez was born and raised in North East Los Angeles, California. She has always been a photographer and now is making her statement as a poet. Her fun and quirky style is one of a kind so take note. While she finishes her studies as an Art Therapist for the youth, her collections are being created and shared at events all across LA. She hopes to raise awareness among those who feel their experiences and emotions are invalid, to create a community where we are all included.

Angel is a queer Zapotec and Honduran person from Koreatown, Los Angeles. They started writing poetry in high school to find a healthy coping mechanism to get through the difficult times they were facing as a queer person of color in the inner-city. They also wanted to have an outlet to express themselves and their beliefs. Through writing poetry they have learned about who they are and what matters to them. Angel wants to focus on writing and other art forms to continue to help themselves and others.

Audrey Kuo is a genderqueer femme poet, writer, bread baker and organizer. Their art is part of their commitment to nurturing relationships and community among queer and trans people of color. Audrey believes in the liberatory possibilities of gathering to share food & stories. Audrey currently lives on unceded Tongva territory (in Los Angeles) and is interested in reconnecting with Taiwanese and Chinese food histories and land.

Hadrian Shawn Miguel (also simply known as, Hadrian) is a multicultural Latinx writer, artist, and poet, born & raised in the Mission barrio of San Francisco who has called New York, Miami, Seattle, and now Los Angeles his home. Their love of storytelling and body of work has given life to over 50 poems, short stories, plays, and songs. The collection of poems here are inspired by modern themes & ideas about sexuality, identity, resilience, family, diversity, and inclusion. Hadrian is influenced by song and rhythms, esp. the music, art, and erotica of Prince's *Dirty Mind, Controversy,* and *1999* era and Madonna's *Sex Book*, and *Erotica & Bedtime Stories* albums.

Jesús Daniel Cruz is a Mexican artist, writer, and poet living in Los Ángeles. The immigrant and gay experience can be discerned in his works. He has worked with the Q-Youth Foundation as an Eastside Queer Stories Festival writer as well as a Pride Poet for the city of West Hollywood and Houses On The Moon theater company as a live storyteller. More of his work and short stories are also available on Amazon Kindle.

Lauren Feller is a Wisconsin native who moved to Los Angeles to escape the frigid Midwest. By day, she works as a copywriter, and enjoys writing everything from marketing copy to melodramatic prose. She also loves pizza, astrology, and her smelly old Shih Tzu.

librecht baker is the author of *vetiver* (Finishing Line Press), an English Professor, and a Sundress Publications' Assistant Editor. She was part of The Vagrancy's 2018-2019 Playwrights' Group and Eastside Queer Stories Festival 2019. baker has attended Ragdale, VONA/Voices, and Lambda Literary Writer's Retreat. she has a MFA from Goddard College. Her poetry appears in *Solace: Writing Refuge, & LGBTQ Women of Color*, Bone Bouquet (Issue 8.1), Sinister Wisdom 107 - Black Lesbians: We are the Revolution!, *Writing the Walls Down: A Convergence of LGBTQ Voices*, and other publications. Baker's play, "Lineage Undone," was awarded Top Performance in the "Top Papers and Performances in Performance Studies" category at Western States Communication Association's 89th Convention.

Lorilyn Luong is an Asian-American Angeleno that pulsates a rainbow heart, goes by she/they pronouns, is a survivor of abuse and has a focus on anti-violence work. Lorilyn believes in the human potential of having a breakthrough after the breakdown, liberating the voice that must speak, and how after the chaos there can be resiliency.

Yessica Avila is a poet and creator who was born in Veracruz, MX and raised in Los Angeles. She enjoys exploring themes of migration and sexuality through various mediums. Their early introduction to the arts has influenced their experimentation in storytelling, digital media, and writing. In addition, Yessica's background in design is an inspiration for the formatting of their poetry. She is currently working as a Communications and Knowledge, Associate and holds a B.F.A in Graphic Design from California State Polytechnic University, Pomona.

Edited by:

Cori Bratby-Rudd (she/her) is a queer LA-based writer and co-founder of Influx Collectiv(e)'s Queer Poetry Reading Series. She graduated Cum Laude from UCLA's Gender Studies department, and received her MFA in Creative Writing from California Institute of the Arts. She has been published in Ms. Magazine, The Gordian Review, Califragile, PANK Magazine, Entropy, Crab Fat Magazine, among others. She won the Editorial Choice Award for her research paper in Audeamus Academic Journal and was nominated as one of Lambda Literary's 2018 Emerging Writers. Her manuscript *Dis/owned* is a semi-finalist for YesYes Book's 2019 Pamet River Prize. You can find her at coribratbyrudd.com.

Ana Bernal (they/them) Executive Director, Organizer & Producer is a Gender Non-Conforming artist born and raised in East Los Angeles. Founder of Q Youth Foundation, a non-profit organization using the power of storytelling to connect the LGBTQIA+ community on the Eastside. They earned a master's degree in Non-Profit Management at Antioch University. Inductee to Honor 41 national list of LGBTQ Latino/a role models for 2015. Currently, they are a professor at Humboldt State University. ana@qyouthfoundation.org